Filled with God's Love

1 Corinthians 13

If I could speak in many different languages and had a beautiful singing voice, but if I didn't speak loving and kind words to those around me...

"Though I speak with the tongues of men and of angels, and have not love..."

(verse 1a)

...My words would sound unpleasant and like ugly noise. It wouldn't make others feel very nice and they'd probably not want to hear me.

"...I am become as a sounding brass or a clanging cymbal."

(verse 1b)

I could be real smart, the best student in my class, and know all there is to know about everything, with A+ and stars all over my papers.

Would people like me then?

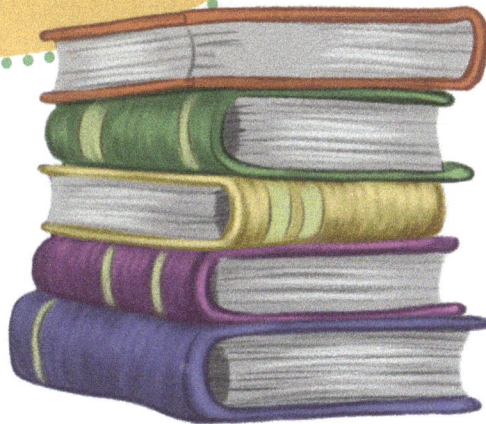

"And though I have the gift of prophecy, and understand all mysteries and all knowledge..."

(verse 2a)

I might be close to God and pray every day. I might have amazing faith to do big impossible things for Him...

"...And though I have all faith, so that I could remove mountains..."

(verse 2b)

...But guess what!
If I'm not a loving
friend, if I am too busy
to think of others, all
the good I do would
mean nothing at all.

"...But don't have love, I am nothing."

(verse 2c)

If I give my extra toys and clothes to poor children who have none, but then don't want to share with my little brother or sister, what good would it do?

"If I share all my goods to feed the poor... but have not love, it profits me nothing."

(verse 3)

Love is being willing
to stop my own game
when someone needs
my help. It's showing
patience, wiping their
tears and helping
them feel better.

"Love is patient
and kind;"

(verse 4a)

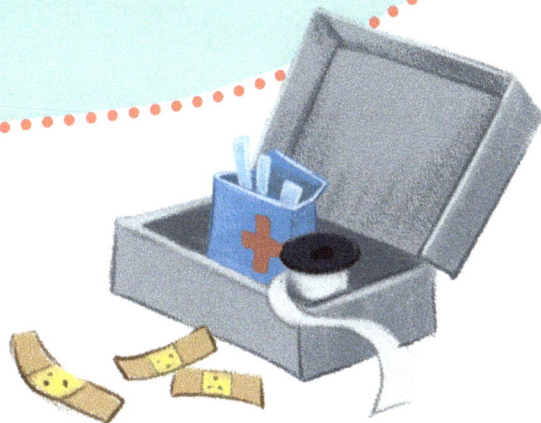

Love is feeling happy for my friends when they get a new toy.

Love is not saying, "Look at what I have that you don't have!"

"Love doesn't envy. Love doesn't think itself to be better than others. Love doesn't boast."

(verse 4b)

Love is not trying
to be the best at
everything. It's working
together as a team to
get things done.

"Love doesn't behave unseemly
and seeks not her own."

(verse 5a)

Love doesn't get upset easily. Love stays kind and forgives even when someone makes a mistake.

"It's not easily provoked, and thinks no evil;"

(verse 5b)

I don't make fun of others or laugh when hurtful things happen to them. With love, I kindly celebrate the good things instead.

"Love doesn't rejoice over iniquity, but rejoices in the truth."

(verse 6)

When I am filled with love, I take care of others and look out for them. I believe in them and encourage them even through difficult times.

"Love bears all things, believes all things and hopes all things. Love endures till the end."

(verse 7)

Things get old, fall, break or get lost, and others may dissapoint me. But there is one thing that I can always count on... LOVE!

"Love never fails."

(verse 8a)

Sometimes when I try my best to work hard and learn new things, it doesn't always work out like I want it to. Life is not always perfect.

"But prophecies, they will fail. Tongues, they will cease. Knowledge, that too will vanish away."

(verse 8b)

There are three important things that I can hold on to: faith, hope and love.

But living with LOVE is the very best thing of all.

"Now abides faith, hope, love, these three; but the greatest of these is love."

(verse 13)

More books in the series:

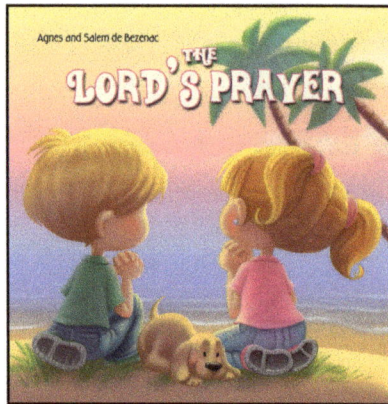

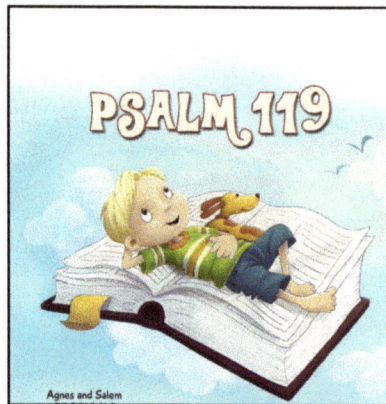

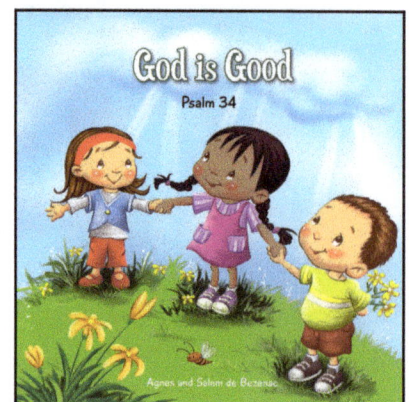

THE LORD'S PRAYER
Agnes and Salem de Bezenac

PSALM 119
Agnes and Salem

SAFE WITH GOD
Psalm 91
Agnes and Salem de BEZENAC

PROVERBS

My Shepherd
Psalm 23
Agnes and Salem de BEZENAC

God is Good
Psalm 34
Agnes and Salem de Bezenac

iCHARACTER

Published by iCharacter Ltd. (Ireland)
www.icharacter.org
By Agnes and Salem de Bezenac
Illustrated by Agnes de Bezenac
Colored by Sporg Studio
Copyright. All rights reserved.
All Bible verses adapted from the KJV.

www.ingramcontent.com/pod-product-compliance
Lightning Source LLC
Chambersburg PA
CBHW040250100426
42811CB00011B/1218